HOW TO TRAIN A PUPPY

A Comprehensive Guide to Raising a Perfect, Obedient and Happy Dog with Simple Basic Commands, Tricks, Skills and Exercises

By American Pet Training Academy

© Copyright 2020 by American Pet Training Academy - All rights reserved.

This eBook is provided with the sole purpose of providing relevant information on a specific topic for which every reasonable effort has been made to ensure that it is both accurate and reasonable. Nevertheless, by purchasing this eBook you consent to the fact that the author, as well as the publisher, are in no way experts on the topics contained herein, regardless of any claims as such that may be made within. As such, any suggestions or recommendations that are made within are done so purely for entertainment value. This is a legally binding declaration that is considered both valid and fair by both the Committee of Publishers Association and the American Bar Association and should be considered as legally binding within the United States.

The reproduction, transmission, and duplication of any of the content found herein, including any specific or extended information will be done as an illegal act regardless of the end form the information ultimately takes. This includes copied versions of the work both physical, digital and audio unless express consent of the Publisher is provided beforehand. Any additional rights reserved.

Furthermore, the information that can be found within the pages described forthwith shall be considered both accurate and truthful when it comes to the recounting of facts. As such, any use, correct or incorrect, of the provided information will render the Publisher free of responsibility as to the actions taken outside of their direct purview. Regardless, there are zero scenarios where the original author or the Publisher can be deemed liable in any fashion for any damages or hardships that may result from any of the information discussed herein.

Additionally, the information in the following pages is intended only for informational purposes and should thus be thought of as universal. Trademarks that are mentioned are done without written consent and can in no way be considered an endorsement from the trademark holder.

TABLE OF CONTENT

DESCRIPTION 7
INTRODUCTION 10
CHAPTER ONE "UNDERSTANDING PUPPIES' PSYCHE & FRIENDLY BEHAVIOR" 14
CHAPTER TWO "INITIAL STEPS FOR TRAINING A PUPPY" 19
CHAPTER THREE "POTTY TRAINING" 29
CHAPTER FOUR "CLEANLINESS & HYGIENE" 38
CHAPTER FIVE "FIVE EASY TRICKS FOR PUPPIES" 48
CHAPTER SIX "CONTROLLING ANGER AND AGGRESSION" 60
CHAPTER SEVEN "OVERCOMING SEPERATION ANXIETY" 71
CHAPTER EIGHT "DIET & NUTRITION" 83
CONCLUSION 91

DESCRIPTION

The book is a comprehensive guide about puppies' training. It provides all the necessary details that are directly or indirectly linked to better grooming of a puppy. The book is formed in form of chapters and each chapter provides several tips and tricks to help you train your dog. To provide a better understanding, the book will start from the basic or initial step and then enhance the significant points.

The chapters are organized to their importance, for example, the first chapter talks about the psyche of puppies and friendly relationship. Everything starts with the mindset and will power, so chapter one is the most salient. Apart from this, to make the book more attractive and engaging, there are bullet points, quotations, studies, and research data. This will promote the interest of the reader in the book and will produce a significant result in puppies' training. Moreover, bullets and sub-headers will save the time of the reader. They can speed-read the essential bullets without going through the entire text. Therefore, this will increase the efficiency of the reader and will give a more productive outcome.

The book is kept simple for the audience to perceive and absorb the information stated. There is no complex sentence structure or vocabulary, and therefore, this book can be read by any person with basic English knowledge. The book includes rhetorical questions to keep the audience attentive throughout the text.

To encourage the reader, there are many different quotations by famous personalities that will ensure the captivity of the reader. These quotations will be a source of inspiration and will become back for lethargic readers. The readers will feel an attachment to the book and will give more care and affection towards their puppies.

"Money can buy you a fine dog, but only love can make him wag his tail." –Kinky Friedman.

INTRODUCTION

Do you like dogs? Or, are you planning to raise a puppy? If yes, then this book is especially for you. It will provide all the necessary information to help to train your new friend. After reading the book, you will not only create a better relationship with your dog, but you will be able to understand the psyche of all the dogs around you.

"Training a puppy is like raising a child. Every single interaction is a training opportunity." –Ian Dunbar.

From the beginning of the human race, dogs and humans have been in a compact and steady relationship. Dogs have been more than friends for their owners. In hard times, they stand beside you and protect you from sorrows, stress, evil, etc. For many people, dogs are like their children. This is because they create a bond, over time, that can't be broken. They become part of your family. Your children play with the dogs, and soon, the love for them is inevitable. Moreover, puppies are a source of entertainment at times of boredom, anxiety, and depression.

We have seen many cases in the past about dogs sacrificing their lives for their owner's safety. From this, it can be learned that dogs are very loyal and loving. They always put their owners at priority rather than their life. Of course, it is not easy to train your dog to such levels, but it is not impossible too. All you need is the right guide to set you on the path that can boost the relationship between your dog and you.

Apart from being loyal and friendly, dogs can help you in your business. Well, this may sound strange to most of you, but dogs do help in several businesses. For example clubs and bars, police, army, etc. have dogs that help them search for illegal items and can help in scanning processes. They can also help you in hunting or at wars. Apart from this, dogs protect their valuables and property. The percentage of robbery is drastically reduced if a dog is present at the spot.

Furthermore, dogs can help you with staying fit and healthy. Imagine that you wake up early and a partner is standing beside your bed to push you towards the morning walks. This will encourage you towards walks and jogs, and eventually, promotes health. Dogs fill the missing element in your life. They become a factor to make your heart stronger and healthier. They push away the stress and depression with their affection and care.

Interestingly, you will become more socialize by having a puppy or a dog. You will become an extrovert with a higher self-efficacy. Have you heard about the dog communities? Well, look up on social media. You get to stay updated about the dog stuff within this community. Apart from this, you get to meet up new people as you visit your nearby park. People that smoke tends to create a bond quicker than a non-smoker. Similarly, dog owners tend to form relation quicker. Soon, you and your dog will have many friends that will bring up-shift in your life.

"I think dogs are the most amazing creatures; they give unconditional love. For me, they are the role model for being alive." –Gilda Radner.

Although dogs provide us with numerous benefits, it is not easy to train one. It requires several strategies, effort, and time to train a puppy or dog as per your requirement. And during this training timeframe, you develop a relationship that has great meaning and affection.

This book is a comprehensive guide to train your dog or puppy as per your needs, so without getting distracted with fake advertisements and academies, let's read out the content to help ourselves and our friend for a training session.

CHAPTER ONE: "UNDERSTANDING PUPPIES' PSYCHE & FRIENDLY BEHAVIOR"

As we have already discussed before, the book is organized in the form of chapters and that each chapter is arranged by priorities. Here, our main priority is comprehending the psychology of Dogs. This chapter is the fundamentals of other chapters and headers. Without gaining knowledge about this division, you will not be able to get mastered in the puppy or dog training. Instead, you will not be able to produce the desired result if you have no grip over natural dog behavior. Interestingly, without this chapter, you will get bored while training your dog. You will be unaware of your dog's actions and reactions. Ultimately, you'll get fed up with the training sessions and lose interest.

What is the psychology of a dog? It is the dog's thinking, actions, operations, and learning. We, humans, are animals too, but we have a verbal language to communicate. We have different psychology than other animals in the world. The human psychologist specializes in the way we think, interpret the world, and dealing with situations. Of course, all this is possible as we have a common way to talk and communicate. However, in the case of dogs, the scenario is way complex. The dogs are unable to talk and they can only express themselves through specific sounds and actions. Moreover, not everyone can interpret their expressions and solve their query. Therefore, we are unable to understand the psychology of the dog.

Dogs are the kindergarten box of crayons. They are simple but diverse. Many people argue that dogs don't have emotions. Well, biologically, they do have emotions as they have the brain to sense and feel. Unlike humans, they have different types of brains and therefore, different behavior, expression, emotions, thoughts, etc.

The main problem in today's dog world is that people want dogs to behave in a physical way like sit, stand, calm, walk, etc., but not focusing on the mind. People need to negotiate with their dogs to encourage and convince them for a certain task or training. Don't bribe them for the task, instead, give them affection at the state of calm and peace. In other words, let them complete the task and then, give them their reward.

If we are talking about humans, we have two ways to think about how other people are thinking: we can either ask them and sometimes they will tell us. Or we can observe actions, behaviors, and we can try to infer things about what people are thinking from their actions. With animals and dogs, of course, we cannot ask them. We don't know what dogs are thinking in a certain moment, and interestingly, they don't know what their thoughts are about. So we can observe their actions, and we can infer their thinking. This is the basis of behaviorism, and it's been around since Pavlov. But there are, of course, very tricky issues here, humans being humans, we tend to anthropomorphize everything.

"And, dog psychology training can help your intelligent dog to become street smart." –Jonathan Trainor.

`The following bullets enlists interesting facts about dog's psychology:

- When a dog barks, it means that either the dog is happy or something unusual or suspicious is going around.

- Dogs become more aggressive if they are walked by a male owner or caretaker. It is thought that dogs might sense the walker's emotion.
- Male dogs appreciate a female playmate, however, female dogs play with both genders.
- It is easy to train a new puppy with an already trained dog. This is because dogs try to adopt the behavior of other dogs. This is referred to as modeling behaviors.
- Dogs don't have developed senses at the time of birth, but after some time, they develop emotions, pain receptors, and senses like humans. However, these senses are not very advanced as that of us.
- Human emotions can become a source of training, so keep a positive ground around your dog to make him more behaved and well-trained. Interestingly, if you take your dog around more, this will boost their behavior senses. Therefore, a dog to a better-organized behavior.
- Some dogs can understand the basic human language. They can sense your actions and reactions. Similar to a child, dogs also learn from their surrounding. So, if you keep a tough and messy environment, your dog will become out-raged and more disobedient.

CHAPTER TWO: "INITIAL STEPS FOR TRAINING A PUPPY"

The domestic dog is ready for consistency, patience, and effective reinforcement. The intention is to instill precise behavior and construct a loving bond together with your pet. It commonly takes around 6 months for a puppy to be fully residence trained, however, some dogs might also take up to a year. Size can be a predictor. For instance, smaller breeds have smaller bladders and higher metabolisms and require extra common journeys outside. Your pup's preceding living conditions are some other predictor. You may find that you want to help your pup break old behavior for you to establish extra ideal ones. And even as you're training, don't fear if there are setbacks. As lengthy as you maintain a control application that includes taking the pup out on the first signal he needs to go and supplying him rewards, he'll learn.

Experts suggest confining the pup to a defined space, whether or not which means in a crate, in a room, or on a leash. As your doggy learns that he needs to move outside to do his business, you can gradually deliver him greater freedom to roam approximately the house. Keep the pup on an everyday feeding schedule and remove his food among meals. Take doggy out to take away the first issue inside the morning after which once every half-hour to an hour. Also, constantly take him out of doors after meals or while he wakes from a nap. Make positive he goes out the final aspect at night and before he's left alone. Take the puppy to the identical spot whenever to do his business. His fragrance will activate him to move. Stay with him outside, at least till he's house trained. When your doggy eliminates outside, praise him or provide him a treat. A walk around the neighborhood is a pleasing reward.

A crate may be a good idea for house education your puppy, at least inside the brief term. It will let you maintain an eye fixed on him for signs he desires to move and educate him to preserve it until you open the crate and allow him outdoor. Make sure it is large enough for the doggy to stand, flip around, and lie down, but not big enough for him to use a corner as a bathroom. If you are the use of the crate for greater than hours at a time, ensure the puppy has clean water, ideally, in a dispenser, you could connect to the crate. If you may not be domestic at some point in the house schooling period, make certain anyone else offers him a break within the center of the day for the primary eight months. Don't use a crate if the pup is doing away within it. Eliminating in the crate could have numerous meanings: he can also have delivered awful habits from the haven or pet save where he lived earlier than; he might not be getting outside sufficient; the crate may be too big, or he may be too younger to preserve it in. Whining, circling, sniffing, barking, or, if your domestic dog is unconfined, barking or scratching at the door, are all signs he desires to move. Take him out proper away. To start on the right foot (and paw!) with your pup, he'll need to recognize what you expect from him. This will make him feel secure in his capability to meet the desires laid out for him going forward.

The foundation of education must be primarily based on high-quality reinforcement. Positive reinforcement is the procedure of giving a canine (or person!) a reward to encourage the conduct you want, like getting a pay take a look at for going to work. The idea isn't to bribe the conduct but to train it the usage of something your dog values. Avoid the usage of punishment together with leash corrections or yelling. Punishment can purpose a canine to end up confused and uncertain about what is being requested of him. It is essential to consider that we can't assume puppies to recognize what they don't know – just like you wouldn't expect a 2-year-old child to understand how to tie his shoes. Patience will go an extended manner in assisting your new pup to discover ways to behave.

Reinforcement may be something your canine likes. Most humans use small portions of a "high cost" meals for schooling treats — something special — which includes dried liver or even just their kibble. Lavish reward or the risk to play with a favorite toy also can be used as a reward. Dogs need to be taught to like rewards. If you deliver the dog a treat while saying "Good dog!" in a glad voice, he'll learn that praise is a good thing and can be a reward. Some puppies also revel in petting. Food is frequently the maximum convenient way to reinforce the behavior.

Puppies can begin quite simple education starting as quickly as they arrive home, commonly round eight weeks old. Always maintain schooling sessions brief — simply 5 to 10 minutes —and continually quit on an effective note. If your pup is having a problem mastering new conduct, cease the consultation by way of reviewing something he already knows and provide him lots of praise and large praise for his success. If your pup receives bored or frustrated, it will ultimately be counterproductive to mastering. You'll want to begin education a recall (come whilst known as) in a quiet location and indoors. Sit together with your puppy and say his call or the word "come." Each time you say "come/call," give your pup a treat. He ought not to do something yet! Just repeat the phrase and supply a treat. Easy!

Next, drop a treat on the floor close to you. As quickly as your doggy finishes the deal with on the ground, say his name again. When he seems up, provide him some other treat. Repeat this a pair of times until you could start tossing the deal with a little similarly away, and he can flip around to stand you whilst you say his name. Avoid repeating your domestic dog's name; saying it too frequently whilst he doesn't respond makes it less difficult for him to ignore it. Instead, move in the direction of your domestic dog and go returned to a step wherein he can be a hit at responding to his name the primary time.

Once your domestic dog can flip round to face you, start including motion and making the sport greater fun! Toss a treat on the ground and take some short steps away at the same time as calling your domestic dog's name. They ought to run after you because the chase is fun! When they capture you, supply them a variety of rewards, treats or play with a tug toy. Coming to you ought to be fun! Continue building on these exercises with longer distances and in other locations. When schooling outside (constantly in a safe, enclosed place), it can be useful to preserve your domestic dog on a long leash at first.

When your puppy is on the verge of coming close to you, don't reach out and take hold of him. This can be perplexing or scary for some puppies. If your pup looks like a bit shy, kneel and face them sideways and offer him treats as you attain for the collar. Never call your dog to punish! This will only train him that you are unpredictable, and it is a superb idea to avoid you. Always praise your canine closely for responding to his or her call, even if they were as much as mischief!

In competition obedience education, "heel" means the dog is strolling in your left facet along with his head even along with your knee even as you maintain the leash loosely. Puppy training may be a little more relaxed with the purpose being that they walk civilly on a free leash without pulling. Some trainers prefer to use the words "let's go" or "ahead" instead of "heel" whilst they train this easy manner of taking walks together.

Whatever cue you choose, be consistent and usually use the identical word. Whether your puppy walks to your left facet or your proper aspect is as much as you. But be steady about in which you need them so they don't get confused and learn how to zig-zag in front of you.

First, ensure your doggy is comfortable wearing a leash. This can look like a bit strange at the beginning, and some puppies might also bite the leash. Give your domestic dog treats as you placed the leash on each time. Then, stand next to for your puppy with the leash in a free loop and supply him several treats in a row for status or sitting next to in your leg. Take one leap forward and encourage him to comply with by giving some other treat as he catches up.

Continue giving treats to your domestic dog at the level of your knee or hip as you walk ahead. When he runs in the front of you, absolutely turn the alternative direction, call him to you, and reward him in the region. Then retain. Gradually begin giving treats similarly apart (from every step to every different step, each third step, and so on). Eventually, your dog will walk fortunately at your aspect each time he's on his leash. Allow your dog lots of time to smell and "smell the roses" on your walks. When they've had their sniffing time, give the cue "Let's Go!" in a happy voice and reward them for coming returned into function and taking walks with you.

There are two different approaches to teach your puppy what "take a seat" means. The first technique is referred to as "capturing". Stand in front of your doggy maintaining some of his dog food or treats. Wait for him to take a seat – say "yes" and give him a treat. Then step backward or sideways to encourage him to stand and watch for him to sit down. Give every other deal with as soon as they take a seat. After a few repetitions, you could begin pronouncing "take a seat" proper as he begins to sit down. The next option is called luring. Get down in front of your pup, protecting a treat as a trap. Put the treat properly in the front of the pup's nose, then slowly lift the meals above his head. He will in all likelihood take a seat as he lifts his head to nibble at the treat. Allow him to consume the treat while his backside touches the floor. Repeat one or two times with the food trap, then do away with the meals and use simply your empty hand, however, hold to praise the domestic dog after he sits. Once he understands the hand signal to take a seat, you can start announcing "take a seat" right earlier than you supply the hand signal. Never bodily put your puppy into the sitting role; this may be puzzling or frightening to some dogs. A puppy who is aware of the "stay" cue will remain sitting until you ask him to get up by way of giving every other cue, known as the "launch phrase." Staying in a region is duration conduct. The goal is to educate your dog to remain sitting until the release cue is given, then begin including distance.

First, educate the release word. Choose which phrase you will use, which include "OK" or "free." Stand along with your pup in a take a seat or a stand, toss a deal with on the ground, and say your phrase as he steps forward to get the deal with. Repeat this a couple of instances till you could say the phrase first after which toss the deal with AFTER he begins to move. This teaches the dog that the release cue manner to move your feet. When your canine knows the discharge cue and the way to sit down on cue, put him in a sit-down, flip and face him, and provide him a treat. Pause, and supply him any other treat for staying in a sit, then launch him. Gradually increase the time you wait between treats (it might help to sing the ABC's to your head and paintings your manner up the alphabet). If your dog receives up earlier than the discharge cue, that's ok! It just method he isn't ready to take a seat for that long so you can make it less difficult by using going returned to a shorter time. Once your canine can stay in a sit for several seconds, you could begin adding distance. Place him in a take a seat and say "live," take one step returned, then step lower back to the pup, give a treat, and your release word. Continue building in steps, maintaining it easy enough that your dog can live a success. Practice each going through him and strolling away along with you're again turned (which is extra realistic).

    Once your dog can live, you may gradually increase the distance. This is also true for the "take a seat." The more solidly he learns this, the longer he can remain sitting. The key is to not count on too much, too soon. Training dreams are achieved in increments so that you can also want to slow down and consciousness on one component at a time. To make sure the education "sticks," sessions have to be short and a success.

"Down" can be taught very in addition to "sit." You can look ahead to your dog to lie down (starting in a boring, small room inclusive of a restroom can assist) and seize the behavior by reinforcing your canine with a treat when he lies down, giving him his launch cue to face lower back up (and encouragement with a lure if needed) and then expecting him to lie down again. When he is quickly mendacity down after standing up, you can begin announcing "down" proper earlier than he does so. You also can entice a down from a sit or stand via retaining a treat in your hand to the canine's nose and slowly bringing it to the ground. Give the treat when the canine's elbows contact the floor to start. After some practices, begin bringing your empty hand to the ground and giving the deal with AFTER he lies down. When he can reliably comply with your hand signal, begin pronouncing "down" as you move your hand. Just like with sitting, by no means use pressure to put your canine into a down. And remember to keep the schooling session quick and fun. End every consultation on an effective note. If you experience your canine is having a difficult time gaining knowledge of or being "stubborn," examine the rate of your education and the fee of your rewards. Do you want to sluggish down and make the steps less difficult, or does your canine want a larger paycheck for a more difficult exercise? The "Basic five" instructions will give your puppy a sturdy basis for any destiny schooling.

CHAPTER THREE: "POTTY TRAINING"

Most dogs are considered puppies for almost two years of age, but to keep a puppy, it's necessary to wait for eight weeks as dog-dog socialization is very important i.e, he is old enough to play with other dogs in puppy class.

Puppy love is a term that can be used in a derogatory fashion, describing emotions which are shallow and transient in comparison to the other forms of love such as romantic love but not for all the people because some people might prefer puppy love on other forms of love so it varies little as well. Puppy love gives some people a new sense of individualism. For the first time, they love someone outside their family. In short, we can say that it is the resemblance to the adoring, worshipful affection that may be felt by a puppy.

For those who love to keep puppies, puppy training is a very important factor. It is necessary to train the puppy necessarily before switching towards the potty training. An eight weeks pup is very different to get trained as compared to a 5-month puppy as some puppies have different manners. Some puppies usually get transformed into a well-trained pup at a very low age, but some take time to meet the expectations. For those who have kept a month puppy, they must need to provide mother feeding to avoid behavioral problems.

Potty coaching your puppy is one in every of the primary and most significant steps a dog owner will fancy brace oneself for a contented, healthy co-existence with their pets. It's vital to try and do analysis before, and certify to formulate an inspiration and schedule supported what quantity time you'll devote to your dog's housetraining. It's also important to supervise your puppy at all times to catch any accidents and keep them out of trouble until they get older.

Firstly, a good rule of thumb is that your puppy will hold their bladder for one hour for each month recently they're. As an example, if the puppy is eight weeks recent, he in all probability can't hold it for extended than two hours. Once they hit twelve weeks, it's around three hours. Puppies will typically hold their bladder for a touch bit longer once they're sleeping (until they wake up) and can go presently when ingestion or taking part in.

If they peep at somewhere then Speaking of punishing, never penalize the puppy for having an accident that they've got it down, mistakes happen. If you yell at them or push their nose in it, your puppy can either learn that they can't eliminate before of you while not going in bothered (so they'll attempt to be sneaky regarding it) or don't have any plan why you're upset and simply get afraid. Keep it positive, reward them for doing it correctly, and easily clean the place and pass on if they need an accident. If you learn to look at rigorously for his or her signs like sniffing around usual, circling, suddenly running over to the corner or another area, etc. you'll be able to catch your puppy before associate degree accident happens.

SOME MAJOR AREAS THAT PLAY A VITAL ROLE IN POTTY TRAINING ARE:

Crates that are a very important puppy housetraining tool that may create your life easier. Puppy pads and paper coaching provide a short-lived answer to housetraining. Consistency, attention, understanding, and patience are all keys in housetraining.

Crate coaching may be an important part of potty coaching success. As den animals, dogs will appreciate crates as a secure area, and as clean creatures, they'll usually need to stay that sleeping area clean but the puppy should be able to stand up and turn around so a crate of the correct size is very important, jointly that's large could convert the pup they need an area to each sleep and eliminate. When used properly, it becomes a secure place they fancy being, thus never use the crate as a penalty. It's okay to administer your puppy breaks or time outs in there, simply build it positive expertise and reward them for stepping into. Puppy pads provide dogs the choice of relieving themselves in an approved spot inside. However, these may be difficult to coach with if you're final goal is to urge the pup to solely potty outside.

Now, we'll discuss crate training a little bit in detail as it is linked with their potty training. So first of all what we have to do is choosing the right crate for the puppy. The crate must be durable, comfortable and flexible at the same time. The crate must be according to the size of a dog. If it is a small puppy then the crate should also be according to the size of the pet. Establishing their mindset and understanding their mood is also very crucial. Make the puppy able to accept the crate as a place to relax. If they are calm they will consider the crate as a place of rest but if they are playing outside then they will prefer to play in a crate as well if you bring them in the crate so things revolve about their mood. Another thing is that to understand the pup's comfort zone. Some folks use dog beds or towels to make a comfortable atmosphere, however, that will not continually be the most effective choice. Depending on the puppy, they'll tear a pup's bed apart or they'll use it to pee on, It's not a nasty factor for them to only sleep on the crate mat itself. Puppies truly do like arduous surfaces some times. Keeping an eye on the puppy will give him more relief and manners at the same time instead of feeling restricted. Puppies need time outside the crate to play, eat and use the bathroom. They don't want to use the place of their sleep to peep but if they don't find any other place to do then they might end up doing there.

As far as pads are concerned, find a suitable place in the home like in stores, laundry or any other place where you can avoid accidents of peep. Give them some corner place instead. Change pee pads usually by placing a tiny low piece of the grungy pad on high of the clean pad within the space you would like your puppy to pee. The scent reminds your puppy that this space is the toilet.

Remove the pee pads nearest to your pet's bed once your puppy is peeing within the same space. Continue removing the pee pads till you have got removed about one or two sheets.

In case of high rise up, puppies create serious problems regarding potty training because they can't be taken out quickly. The first thing is the pee pad that is an easy precaution. If you are at some other place like you are at your friend's place then it is easy to take pee pads and puppy along with you because they are easily movable. If you think that your puppy has dropped it on the floor then clean it and move your puppy onto the pee pad. One more thing we can do is to put a grass patch on your terrace. Their square measure has many corporations that may mail you a patch of sod for your puppy to try and do their business on. Some square measure simply patches of grass have containers to place the waste in so you'll empty any waste which may drain out. Get a puppy's waste instrumentality to place any poop luggage in therefore it doesn't linger and smell, then simply empty the instrumentality once it's full. Making the puppy punctual can provide you ease. Eventually, your puppy will be able to hold it long enough to induce them down the steps or elevator and outdoors whereas you will need to stay pee pads or your grass patch around for times after you can't (or don't need to) leave, it will facilitate your puppy to induce on a schedule for once they square measure speculated to eliminate. After you get a young puppy, attempt to take them out as usual as possible: within the morning once they stand up, when breakfast/before you permit for work, at lunch period, after work, when dinner, before bed, etc. As they become old, you will be able to depart with a schedule like before and when to work and before bed.

While it should at the start desire a frightening task, with a bit preparation and consistency, house coaching your dog in an exceeding high-rise isn't that a lot of totally different than anyplace else.

Weather also affects the pet if it is too cold or too hot then you have to take measures accordingly. For example, teach him to go quickly on cue and not stay too long in the cold, clear a regular path, and possibly mark his regular spot to make trips quicker, adjust his schedule in winter to time potty breaks for good weather.

For the first step or this, initial you ought to be ready to require your puppy out on her potty break quickly. Have everything, as well as the leash, poop-bags, heat covering for each of you, etc prepared earlier. Pushing off on chores will appear a true medicinal drug within the cold, and being ready earlier helps thaw enthusiasm an honest deal. Don't play or ramble around, and go straight for elimination once you depart. Use a command like "Go potty" whenever your pup eliminates also will facilitate quicken things eventually. And keep in mind to treat and show affectionateness whenever your pup goes quickly or goes on command. Having a frequently cleared and maintained path to your pup's regular elimination spot can extremely facilitate speed things on, too. For the spot itself, keep it afar from snow or ice as close to the bottom as attainable, with space for your pup to show and sniff around. The scent of previous eliminations is probably the simplest cue for dogs, and keeping the spot clear can facilitate. To make journeys easier, attempt to alter your pup's feeding and walking schedules for the winter to times once the weather is nice. For instance, you'll be able to time multiple journeys throughout the day, particularly at or close to midday once it's hotter, and build it so dinner is previous in summer. But detain mind that mealtimes can be adjusted too, for puppies eliminate pretty shortly once intake. You will conjointly keep an in-depth eye on your pup for all the signals throughout the adjusting amount and teaching his/her a proof-like ringing a bell close to the door once he/she needs to travel is also useful.

One more thing which is important is that when you identify the routine of taking your puppy out once sleeping, eating and taking part in, you furthermore may specialize in what to try and do once you're outside.

Find a spot that will become the "potty spot", and invariably take your dog to a similar spot. Stand quietly and wait till they're prepared, and as they start, provide a voice command or signal to "go potty" or "do your business." Then await the results, and praise lavishly if your puppy goes. Say "good boy/girl!" then provide the pup a pleasant-tasting treat.

In the end, I will conclude that puppies are the sweetest creatures and they learn everything in the exact way how you teach them or how you handle them. If you are tackling them with anger then they tackle everything and every other man with anger and that's not a good sign. Peep is an accident that shouldn't be called an accident but still, we call it though. Puppies don't have a brain and they will try to keep themselves in ease in the best possible way without thinking so you are the caretaker and you have to teach them and if you get succeeded in doing so then they will also feel reluctant to do the thing that you are not allowing them.

CHAPTER FOUR: "CLEANLINESS & HYGIENE"

Getting your dog tidy often is vital, and going away it to the consultants is crucial. It's false to require your dog daily for knowledgeable grooming, however, it's sensible to grasp that what to do and what to avoid for maintaining your dog's hygiene and cleanliness up to the mark. Puppies are like humans. They have traits like humans do possess like being loyal to the others most importantly to the owner, as we feel uncomfortable when we are unhealthy or feeling unconscious so we consult doctors because we can't live with everlasting even temporary health problem but we have the patience to face it. The same is the case with the dogs, their behavior shows us that they are feeling uncomfortable so we have to point out the problem. In the case of cleanliness, we are concerned about it but puppies are not. The caretaker has to work on it. We can't remain unclean for so long because this results in the subsequent diseases and so is in the case of dogs/puppies. The difference is that we feel for it but they don't. They can remain untidy but to make them look good we wash them and make them presentable and also to preserve them from diseases.

We are going to talk about their health and cleanliness not only about their looks but also their food because food is also a crucial factor in their clean nature. First of all, we will discuss bathing them. Bathing is very important for their healthy skin and a healthy coat. This removes the unpleasant odor or any dirt that they have accumulated. This helps in removing their loose hairs, debris and improving their coat's shine. Bathing can be used as their medical treatment as well but take care of doctor's recommendations as well. Giving them too much bath can also cause skin problems for them. This can dry out their skin and coat can also cause problems. If you notice an associate unpleasant odor from your dog, this might be caused by rolling in one thing that smells unpleasant, however, if you can't determine associate external cause your dog ought to be checked by a vet to rule out any medical causes of an unpleasant smell like skin or ear issues. One thing that we must concern about is that we don't use human products like shampoo that made for human's skin because puppy's skin is very sensitive even in case of dogs so products vary from body to body of species so don't use them for puppies. For dogs with healthy skin and coat, opt for a light and delicate hypoallergenic shampoo. For dogs with skin conditions, your native vet will advise what form of shampoo or product to use to assist manage or treat specific skin issues. You can conjointly strive to apply light and delicate hypoallergenic rinse-out conditioner when shampooing to assist stop status when shampooing. Initially test the product to create positive there's no reaction or irritation. If your dog appears irritated in the slightest degree – see your vet and take a look at a special product that doesn't cause any irritation.

In the case of outdoors, if we are taking the puppy outside and want to clean it there then or want to bath them, then we should find a suitable hose. As we are talking about puppies so it is easy to lift them, so bathing them is also very easy. In case of cold weather, we have to take the temperature and pressure of water into consideration as well. Warm water is very suitable for puppies as compared to cold water in winter. They quite feel reluctant in cold water in winters so must take care of it as well.

THE NECESSARY STEPS THAT ARE REQUIRED FOR THEIR BATHING ARE DISCUSSED BELOW:

Train your puppy in such a way that he/she allows you to give him gentle pushes like patting, stroking, etc. Go slowly, patting them on there all the body like from chest area, shoulders, sides, to the back. One they get comfortable, try to lift their paws and move hands on their nails. This will make your puppy react less when you will bath them.

Now as we know that dogs are very sensitive to the equipment that we use while bathing them so introduce the equipment simultaneously. Start by introducing your dog to the tub instrumentality you're about to use, one item at a time like towels, buckets, shampoo containers, and hoses. Practice standing on the non-slip mats and reward your dog for standing on the mat. you'll be able to conjointly follow standing within the tub however while not exploitation any water, this manner your dog will step by step get won't be within the tub. Reward with treats whereas within the tub.

You can conjointly activate the hose and faucet once your dog is near so they'll see and listen to the running water. Being introduced to bath-related things step by step in a very positive and calm manner is that the best thanks to training your dog.

SOME OTHER USEFUL TIPS WHILE CLEANING THEM ARE THE FOLLOWING:

Gently brush your dog's coat each alternative day to forestall knotting and matting, and to assist management shedding. Wipe any outside detritus from canine's coat with a moist towel as before long as you notice it. Survey your dog's body for ticks often, particularly in hotter months. Check your dog's paws often to ensure rocks, thorns, or other irritants aren't embedded in them. Keep your dog's nails cut so that they don't get caught on something leading to an injury. Carefully trim hair that covers your dog's eyes if they're a breed prone to this characteristic. Wipe the within of your dog's ears weekly with a damp plant disease. Wrap gauze around your finger and wipe your dog's teeth many times per week to stay food buildup at a minimum.

We can't limit it to useful do's but we have to point out something that we can't do because this will cause our dogs to get irritated or might result in some other things that we don't want. For example, try not to treat any injuries you notice yourself. Don't try to clip your dog's fur yourself. An expert is aware of how long a dog's fur ought to be and has special techniques for trimming around sensitive areas. Try not to attempt to clip the puppy's nails if you're not snug and educated concerning doing, therefore. Clipping them too short will cause extreme pain. Don't cut matted fur out of your dog's coat yourself. Use "human" beauty and hygiene products on your canine unless approved by your vet, or groomer. Don't bathe your dog in a very bath, or shower, if he gets panic around water. Your dog may injure you and/or her/himself. Don't bathe your dog outdoors in cool, or cold, weather. His or her vital signs will drop speedily in these conditions. Don't commit to taking away foreign objects from your dog's eyes, ears, nose, or mouth yourself. Consult your MD. Don't spray a malodorous canine with perfumes, or fragranced products. A dog's sense of smell is extraordinarily sensitive and this may cause him or her distress and discomfort.

Teeth and nails are very sensitive parts of their body. Someone professional or experienced is better to do instead of the beginner. Dogs have 2 styles of nails, spurs, and toenails, that square measure perpetually growing. Toenails ought to wear naturally, however, if they grow tons, they need to be cut. All puppies would like correct nail care. In general, puppies don't ought to have their nails cut, however, if you hear the noise the nails build on the bottom, you'll cut them. Raise the vet to point out the simplest techniques.

Keeping your dog's fur, teeth, nails, skin, ears, eyes, and paws clean is good for him or her as well as for your sense of smell. When it comes to brush and comb the puppy we notice that outside dogs strip off their fur twice in a calendar year whereas indoor dogs usually puppies lose fur throughout the year. So bathing them and brushing their hair helps them to lose fur. That thing also depends on how healthy the coat of puppy is. The fur of puppies usually varies from short to medium and then to large fur. In the case of short fur. Although short fur doesn't need such frequent cleansing, it's necessary to brush it from time to time. To loosen dead skin and fur, you must brush within the other way of fur growth with a top-quality dog brush. Then, you'll be able to take away the residues with a brush within the direction of fur growth throughout the body. Finally, leave the shiny coat with a humid suede. In case of puppy grooming with medium hair, These dogs ought to be brushed additional times, a minimum of once every week, because of the density of their fur, which consists of a sub-layer and a higher layer. Use a barbed brush and comb against the expansion of the fur, to loosen the maximum amount of dead hair and skin as attainable and peel the sub-layer. Then, you'll use a brush to comb within the direction of fur growth and take away rubble.

A wide-toothed comb may be used on the tail and legs. The fur of hard-haired dogs ought to be removed four to 5 times a year, with a baring blade and thumb. This is often not in the least painful if wiped out the proper means, within the direction of hair growth.

Variations that occur in case of long hairs of pups we know that Although they're stunning, long coatings need daily brushing. This could take up to Associate in a Nursing hour each day within the case of Afghan hounds, as an example. Use a barbed brush and comb within the direction of fur growth, to loosen knots and tangles. As a result of the coat is long, comb it will pull the skin, therefore care should be taken to avoid pain the puppy. The use of a brush on dogs with satiny furs, like geographic region terriers and Afghan hounds, can add shine to the fur. A wire brush may be accustomed to take away impurities from dog's fur with Associate in Nursing plentiful sub-layer, like hairy collies. A wide-tooth comb may be accustomed to detangle the hair behind the hocks. All cleansing tools ought to be cleansed and hold on during a dry place once every use. To stop the wire brushes from oxidation, clean them well and rub them with a fabric soaked in edible fat.

Some other cares like their eyes like dirt in their eyes cause problems for them to sleep so take necessary precautions. Use cotton, clean and warm water to remove any dirt with soft hands. Puppies have two types of ears, dropped and raised. Dropped ears should be examined more carefully as the ear canal is less ventilated. In the case of teeth, the redness around teeth is a sign of inflammation so use proper brush designed for dogs to keep them prevent from harm.

When it comes to food that they eat we know that usually diseases spread out by unhygienic food. Today in modern world food has lost its purity when it comes to developing or under developing countries. Dedicated puppy lovers are usually very kind as well. The food like fruits and vegetables that we can easily digest can cause severe health problems when get eaten up by little puppies or even dogs as well. Not in all cases because some of the food that humans eat can also be very useful when getting eaten up by the puppies. This provides them joint strength, better breath, and allergy immunity. Food that is being eaten by human-like bread, cashews(if taken with precautions like not too salty that dogs don't love we can give them by keeping limit), then we can give them cheese which is very useful for their health, coconut having lauric acid help them to fight bacteria and viruses, corn, eggs, fish, ham, honey which is a source of many nutrients vitamins A, B, C, D, E, and K, potassium, calcium, magnesium, copper, and antioxidants, then milk which is a big source of strength but take care of one thing that some dogs even puppies are intolerant and don't digest milk well, then we can add peanut butter, peanuts, popcorn, pork, quinoa, salmons, tuna, turkey, wheat/grains, yogurt as well. Stay them away from almonds that they can make problems for their digestive tract if not get digested easily. Dogs should never eat chocolate as they contain toxic substances like methylxanthines that can disturb their metabolic process, others like cinnamons, icecream you should avoid giving them.

In the end, I can conclude that dogs are a very friendly and loyal creature of god and they should be treated by full care and knowledge about things that you will give a use for them, equipment, food, techniques, etc.

CHAPTER FIVE: "FIVE EASY TRICKS FOR PUPPIES"

SETTING UP FOR THE TRICK

1. Make sure your dog knows the way to lie. This is often an important initiative for completing the rollover trick since the dog has got to be lying right down to perform it. If your dog doesn't answer the "lie down" command, train him to try to that first. You can also start by letting your dog lie on his side. This might help him initially learn to roll over.
2. Have some treats available. Give your dog treats that he doesn't normally get, like lean luncheon meat (roast beef, ham, or turkey), cheese, store-bought dog treats, chicken, or another food your dog loves. Break the treats into small bites to form them last through the training session and keep your dog from filling up too fast. Keeping your dog hungry for treats is going to keep him focused and motivated to find out to roll over. Avoid any high salt or fatty foods. If you'd rather not feed your dog treats, you can use a verbal phrase. However, a more precise thanks to the train is with a clicker and treats. You'll get to train the clicker first. The clicker is beneficial because you'll click at the precise second the dog modifies behavior. This is often more precise than verbal praise or simply

giving treats. The dog associates the noise with a treat (which you'll give to him/her a couple of seconds later). Clicker train your dog first and once he associates the noise as a gift, you will start training him to roll over Never use punishment as to how to coach your dog. Dogs don't understand negative reinforcement and that they won't learn new tricks as a result of it. Negative tones or forcing him to perform tricks might cause your dog to associate the trick with feeling negative sensations like fear.

3. Move to a good training room. When you're training your dog, it's good to start in a room that's comfortable and free of most distractions. Choose a room with plenty of floor space, since the dog will be moving around quite a bit. Once your dog learns how to do the trick in the comfort of his home, he'll be able to do it outdoors or in public. Let other people in the house know what you're doing, so they won't distract the dog during the training session.

THE FIVE TRICKS ARE MENTIONED BELOW:

1. THE ROLLOVER
   - Give your dog the command to "lie down." Your dog should start the "rollover" trick during lying down position, resting on his stomach alongside his paws before him and his head lifted. From this position, he'll be able to roll over easily and without hurting himself.

- Hold a treat near the dog's face. Slump and hold a treat where the dog can see and smell it, on the brink of his face. Close your fingers around the treat to make sure he is unable snatch it from your hand before the trick is completed.
- If your dog tends to grab treats quickly, inform to observe your fingers so you don't get a bit.
- Move the treat and say, "rollover." Rotate the treat up and around your dog's head so that his nose follows the treat. Where the nose goes, the highest and body will usually follow. If you lead your dog's nose with the treat along a path that can cause your dog to roll over as he follows it, your dog will rollover. Say, "rollover" during a transparent and friendly voice while you progress the treat around the side of his head.
- The keys to urge your dog to associate the spoken command with the physical move of rolling over. If you prefer, you'll use a hand signal by making a rolling motion alongside your hand. Otherwise, you'll provide a verbal and physical signal simultaneously.
- Help your dog and keep practicing. Use your blank check to softly help your dog roll over if he's almost getting the advance his own. Practice the trick repeatedly because this may be a difficult move for a dog to make. As you practice reward your dog with a treat as he

makes moves within the proper direction. This might encourage him to remain trying.
- Your dog might get frustrated if you wait to reward him until he rolls over completely. Don't forget to praise your dog during a sort, excited voice. Dogs respond positively to a stimulating "good boy or good girl."
- Know when to reward your dog. At first, reward your dog with a treat and praise whenever he successfully rolls over. The repeated rewards will reinforce this acquired behavior. Once he knows what you expect, you'll give treats less frequently
- Reward your dog immediately, within few seconds after taking the proper action. This might help your dog know what he's doing right so that he can repeat it.
- Keep practicing until he can do the trick without help. After the first, small successes, the dog should be able to roll over without your help. You got to not need to move the treat over his head or physically roll his body over. Rise and tell him to roll over; when he does so on his own, reward him with a treat and a pat on the highest.

PRACTICING THE TRICKS

- Practice until the dog can roll over without having a treat. Once your dog knows what you expect once you say "roll over," change the way you treat your dog. Don't offer a treat whenever. Slowly stretch out the time between treats and gradually give random or less appealing treats. This might keep your dog from expecting a treat every single time he rolls over. Keeping it unpredictable also will keep your dog inquisitive about performing the trick.

- Continue rewarding with verbal statements (like "good boy") and affectionate petting. Save the special treats for the next trick you wish to point out your dog and instead, give him less desirable treats, like store-bought treats or pieces of pet food.
- Practice in new locations with distractions. At now, you'll be wanting to introduce a replacement practice location. This might still challenge your dog and stop him from only associating the new trick with the training room. Start practicing outside, first with a treat, then without. A dog park could also be an excellent spot to practice, with many distractions.
- Your dog could even be challenged by the new distractions. Twiddling my thumbs with him and reintroduce treats until he consistently rolls over in new locations.
- Move on to practicing around people. Practicing before people will let him get used to performing. The extra praise he'll get from people also will encourage him to roll over. Try

letting people give him the "rollover" command. When your dog truly has the trick down, he might roll over when somebody else gives him the command.

2. TEACHING DOGS SHAKE

When you start teaching shake, ensure to possess plenty of high-value treats or rewards. Or, if you prefer, a clicker. The following steps will assist you easily teach your dog because of shake hands:

- Hold your arm out to your dog.
- Your dog may do some experimenting to work out what you would like, like sniffing, licking, etc. The key to attend it out, not saying anything. As soon as your dog paws at your hand, click/praise, open your hand and provides the treatment.
- Repeat the above step several times until the dog shows that he is consistently pawing at your hand.
- Once this behavior seems to be solidly "acquired", start building the duration and increasing the matter. Has your dog held their paw on your hand for slightly longer before you praise/click and treat? Remember, you aren't giving any verbal cues to your dog yet. You'd wish to make sure that your dog completely understands the trick before adding within the

formal cue. This might help avoid confusion or accidentally teaching your dog to paw at you rather than shaking your hand.
- Start slowly with building duration when your dog paws at your hand. Wait until your dog's paw rests on your hand before clicking/praising and treating. You would like to form sure that your dog understands what you would like is their paw on your hand, therefore the timing of treating and praising is vital.
- Ask your dog to carry their paw on your hand first for less than for a second before clicking/praising and treating. Your dog will find out that what gets the treat isn't just scratching at you, but placing their paw on your hand.
- When your dog is consistently placing their paw on your hand, start introducing a verbal cue of your choice. "The shake" is that the commonest cue, but you'll use any word you would like. Once you hold out your hand right before your dog's paw makes contact, say "shake," then praise/click and treat. You would like your dog to form the association between the "shake" behavior and therefore the verbal cue. Again, timing is vital. You would like to start out introducing the verbal cue right before your dog offers the "shake" behavior, and once you are confident your dog goes to shake your hand.

- When your dog is almost always successful at this level, you'll flatten your hand sideways and hold it bent your dog, asking them to shake by using your verbal cue. When your dog's paw meets your hand, click/praise and treat. If your dog doesn't shake at that time, it just means they aren't quite ready for this step. When your dog is consistently ready to place their paw on your outstretched hand, you'll start to introduce some gentle movement up and down. Remember to praise and treat for this too. If at any point your dog becomes nervous or uncertain, just copy to the previous step where they were successful, work that a couple of times, then slowly re-introduce the tougher step.

3. HIGH FIVE

    As your dog masters the "shake" command, it is a simple interest to teach him to try to a "high five. "Start by performing on the "shake" command, but begin to carry your palm out and because the dog hits your palm, give the command "high five." Treat and praise your dog immediately. Your goal here is to urge the dog to boost its paw as high as possible and to touch your open palm.

4. "Start by performing on the "shake" command, but begin to carry your palm out and because the dog hits your palm, give the command "high five."

"Start by performing on the "shake" command, but begin to carry your palm out and because the dog hits your palm, give the command "high-five." Start by getting your dog excited by tossing a ball or talking in an excited tone. Then, put your dog during a "sit" position and wave a treat by your dog's nose. Keep waving the treat without letting him see it until your dog whines or cries. As soon as he makes a sound, reward your dog with the treat.

Repeat the method, but use the command "speak" as your dog begins to form noise. Do not reward your dog until it makes noise. And always tell your dog "hush" or "enough" and walk off once you want your dog to prevent.

Note: If your dog features a tendency to bark excessively, use this trick only your dog is during a sitting position. Barking at everything that walks by your front window shouldn't be encouraged and will never be rewarded with treats or praise.

5. DANCE

    Although almost any dog is often taught to bop, the smaller breeds are typically easier to coach. Getting a Saint Bernard abreast of its hind legs is often challenging, but lively dogs under 40 pounds can quickly learn to chop a rug.

Start together with your dog during a sitting position and hold a treat in your closed hand near its nose. Slowly lift your fork over and slightly behind the dog's head therefore the dog looks back and begins to face on its hind legs. As soon as your dog stands on its hind legs, praise the dog and provides it the treat. Repeat the method until your dog stands quickly and sturdily on its back legs.

Then, begin moving the treat above the dog's head during a small circle. You want your dog to twirl on its hind legs. As soon because the dog begins to step during a circle, use the term "dance" and offer praise and therefore the treat. Use the treat as bait to urge the dog to face up and switch during a circle. Again, this trick is simpler to accomplish with small, agile dogs. Avoid this trick if you've got a breed susceptible to back trouble like a dachshund.

Teaching your dog a couple of simple tricks is fun and entertaining for both of you. it is best if your dog knows (and can reliably perform) the essential obedience commands of sit, stay and down before advancing to tricks. Most tricks are built on these commands and your dog will have learned to concentrate on you during training sessions.

If your dog has any sort of arthritis or degenerative joint disease, ask your veterinarian before proceeding.

Even simple tricks can place stress on joints that are painful and sore.

The success of coaching your dog relies on rewarding correct behavior. Rewards differ from dog to dog; for a few, it's going to be food and for others praise. Some dogs will do whatever you would like just to possess a touch playtime. Find the reward that best motivates your dog to find out. Work together with your dog daily in 5 to fifteen-minute sessions. Keep it fun and end the session with a gift.

CHAPTER SIX: "CONTROLLING ANGER AND AGGRESSION"

Science has progressed a protracted, great distance beyond the thinking of Descartes and Malebranche. we've now come to grasp that dogs possess all of the identical brain structures that produce emotions in humans. Dogs have identical hormones and undergo identical chemical changes that humans do during emotional states. Dogs even have the hormone oxytocin, which, in humans, is involved feeling love and affection for others.

With identical neurology and chemistry that folk has, it seems reasonable to suggest that dogs even have emotions that are almost like ours. However, it's important to not go overboard and immediately assume that the emotional ranges of dogs and humans are identical.

To understand what dogs feel, we must intercommunicate research done to explore the emotions of humans. It's the case that not all people have the complete range of all possible emotions, and, in fact, at some points in your life you probably did not have the complete complement of emotions that you simply feel and express today. There's much research to demonstrate that infants and young children have a more limited range of emotions. It's overtime that the infant's emotions begin to differentiate and develop and, by the time they've reached adulthood, their range of emotional experiences is sort of broad.

Why is such data important to understanding the emotional lives of our dogs? Researchers have now come to believe that the mind of a dog is roughly such as that of an individual who is two to two-and-a-half years old. This conclusion holds for many mental abilities likewise as emotions. Thus, we will look at human research to determine what we would expect of our dogs. A bit like a two-year-old child, our dogs have emotions, but many fewer sorts of emotions than found in adult humans.

At birth, an individual's infant-only has an emotion that we would call excitement. This means how excited he's, starting from very calm up to a state of frenzy. Within the primary weeks of life, the joy state involves tackle a varying positive or a negative flavor, so we will now detect the overall emotions of contentment and distress. Within the next few months, disgust, fear, and anger become detectable within the infant. Joy often doesn't appear until the infant is sort of six months old and it's followed by the emergence of shyness or suspicion. True affection, the type that it is smart to use the label "love" for, doesn't fully emerge until nine or ten months old.

The complex social emotions—those which have elements that have got to be learned— don't appear until much later. Shame and pride take close to three years to look, while guilt appears around six months then. A toddler is sort of four years old before she feels contempt. Aggression isn't breed-specific. When sweet, loving, friendly dogs exist in every breed, so do aggressive dogs. No single breed is an exception. It is your responsibility to be open-minded once you see a tangle. Meaning taking immediate and appropriate action, at any sign of aggression. The illusion that things will change is not the solution.

The first thing you must do is speak to your veterinarian. Has your veterinarian examine your puppy? There may well be medical issues. There may well be genetic issues, or there could even be other pressing matters that need to be addressed as soon as possible. The longer you wait, the harder it would be to correct.

Unless there is a severe genetic or neurological problem, the younger a puppy is, the higher it's to modify their inappropriate behaviors. Often puppy fear can become puppy aggression. Positive reinforcement, punishment-free obedience training may be a method to create a well-behaved, well-mannered dog. Understanding the thanks to teaching a dog social skills is critical.

The most common aggressive puppy warning signs include snarling, growling, mounting, snapping, nipping, lip curling, lunging, dominance, challenging stance, dead-eye stare, aggressive barking, possessiveness, and after all, biting! Watch your puppy's behavior around areas where there's food. Early signs of aggression in puppies include being possessive over toys and food.

Is your puppy protective of his food bowl? How does he or she growl or snarl as you walk by their food bowl while they're eating? Do they growl or snap after you reach for his or her food bowl, whether or not it's empty? Do they snatch treats or food out of your hand? Does your puppy lunge, growl, or snap, as you try to retrieve a dropped piece of food? Are they protective of the trash container?

In other rooms of the house, does your puppy assert a claim to any specific piece of furniture, like a chair, couch or bed? Is your puppy possessive of toys or other items, especially items which may belong to your children?

How does the puppy act when someone, especially someone they don't know, walks into the house or enters a room? Does the puppy react differently when an unfamiliar child involves the house?

Does the puppy exhibit an unusually high prey drive, by chasing and nipping at anything that's moving? Do they over-react aggressively to playful teasing, sudden movements, being awakened from a deep sleep, or when being corrected? Or are they unwilling to be touched?

Also, watch how your puppy reacts to other dogs and puppies. Does your puppy attempt to dominate other puppies or adult dogs? That kind of early aggression possesses to be curbed immediately with training.

TEETHING, NIPPING, AND BITING

You must know the difference between puppy teething, puppy nipping, and puppy biting.

PUPPY TEETHING: When puppies are teething, their mouths hurt which they are going to bite or chew in an attempt to alleviate that pain. Give your dog appropriate chew toys.

PUPPY NIPPING: If your dog playfully nips at you but doesn't break the skin, you simply must look out to remain playtime from getting too rough. After 15 weeks, your puppy shouldn't attempt to touch your skin beside his teeth. If he continues to undertake to nip or bite you then time, you'd wish to use training to stop that behavior. Never hit a puppy that bites. And don't bite back. Instead, when your puppy gets too rough, stop playtime and go forth. Your puppy should quickly learn that you simply just will ignore him if he misbehaves.

PUPPY BITING: It's time to induce concerned if your puppy bites lots or tries to bite you whenever you touch the dog. If your puppy aggressively or viciously tries to bite or if a snarl or growl accompanies the attempt to bite, you'd wish to wish action. It's also dangerous if your puppy tries to bite your face or if your puppy tries to bite other dogs, or others, especially children. When the puppy has become aggressive about biting, especially if the bites break the skin and cause bleeding, it's a sign the dog is trying to be dominant.

HOW TO STOP AGGRESSION

Make a note of when your dog becomes aggressive and therefore the circumstances surrounding the behavior. This may play a crucial part in determining your next step. It's essential to affect the underlying explanation for the aggression. The behavior is simply a symbol of an underlying problem. There are varieties of the way you'll manage the hostility and help your dog remain calm. It'll take time, consistency, and possibly the assistance of knowledgeable. See Your Veterinarian. Dogs that are not normally aggressive but suddenly develop aggressive behaviors may need an underlying medical problem. Health problems that will cause aggression include hypothyroidism, painful injuries, and neurological problems like encephalitis, epilepsy and brain tumors. Talk to your veterinarian to work out whether this is often the case together with your dog. Treatment or medication may make big improvements in your dog's behavior. Call in a Professional if your vet has ruled out a medical problem, it is time to call in a professional dog trainer or animal behaviorist. Because aggression is such a significant problem, you should not plan to fix it on your own. Knowledgeable can assist you to find out what's causing your dog's aggression and make an idea to manage it.

Knowledgeable can assist you to find out what's causing your dog's aggression and make an idea to manage it. A behaviorist or trainer can assist you to find out the simplest approach for managing your dog's aggression. In most cases, you'll use positive reinforcement to show your dog new behaviors. For example, if your dog is mildly aggressive toward strangers, begin by standing distant from someone your dog doesn't know. You ought to be far enough away so that your dog doesn't start to growl or snap. Then, reward with many treats and praise as you gradually decrease the space between your dog and therefore the stranger, continuing to use positive reinforcement.

Ideally, your dog will begin to find out that strangers equal treats and you will see a discount in its aggression. This same procedure can work for getting your dog won't to a spread of other situations.

AVOID PUNISHMENT

Punishing your dog for aggressive behavior usually backfires and may escalate the aggression. If you answer a growling dog by hitting, yelling or using another aversive method, the dog may feel the necessity to defend itself by biting you. Punishment can also cause your dog biting somebody else all of sudden. For instance, a dog that growls at children is letting you recognize that he's uncomfortable around them. If you punish a dog for growling, he might not warn you about the subsequent time he gets uncomfortable, but may simply bite. Reactive dogs must not ever be punished! Punishing dogs for being reactive is punishing their reaction to being frightened and uncomfortable then it'll only make them more scared. It does nothing to treat the explanation for why they act reactively. Punishing reactive dogs has been proven to worsen the condition and anxiety and destroy the bond between the dog and human. Remember, reactive dogs are fearful dogs and that we got to determine why and make them feel less scared to scale back the behavior. When people punish dogs, they're usually trying to show them what's right and wrong but dogs aren't moral creatures and to them, there's no "right and wrong" just "good and bad" in terms of consequences of their actions to themselves.

THERE'S AN EXTENDED LIST OF REASONS WHY PUNISHMENT SHOULD NEVER BE USED SUCH AS:

- It worsens anxiety and reactive behavior.
- It does nothing to deal with the underlying emotion or help the dog.
- It can inhibit the first warning signs of reaction like growling leadingly a dog to escalate its reaction and bite more readily.
- It destroys the bond and trust between the dog and human.
- It does nothing to show the dog how it should be behaving.
- It is worth mentioning that for punishment to be effective it must fulfill 3 criteria:

- IMMEDIATE (Occur within half a second of the undesirable behavior.)
- CONSISTENT (happen whenever the behavior occurs - which must include when the owner is absent)
- AVERSIVE (unpleasant enough to prevent the behavior permanently after 1 or 2 manifestations).

If these criteria aren't fulfilled then by definition it's not punishment but ABUSE. Needless to mention, proper punishment is impossible to try to correctly and fairly, and there are always more humane ways of altering behavior. Punishment is nearly never recommended or needed for any animal in any circumstance. Consider Medication.

In some instances, training alone isn't enough. Dogs that are aggressive due to fear may have medication to assist manage the matter. It is vital to know that a dog experiencing fear, stress, or anxiety is incapable of learning new things. Consider medication as a tool to assist your dog overcomes this fear. Many dogs will only need medication temporarily. Ask your veterinarian about your options to handle unavoidable situations.

Finally, you would like to think about whether your lifestyle allows you to stay with an idea. As an example, if you've got a dog that acts aggressively towards children and you've got kids, it's impossible to avoid things that bring out the aggression. During this case, the simplest option for you and your dog could also be finding it a replacement home with adults only.

Moreover, Dogs are very territorial and very tuned into the hierarchy of a group. Dominance is very important in a canine society. Most of the behavior problems you have with your dog may stem from the way your dog perceives the power structure with you. If your dog believes he is the "top dog" or "alpha male" in your house, he might try to assert his dominance over you. For this reason, they can be motivated to fight, and when dogs fight, it can be quite frightening and dangerous for all involved. Summarizing the chapter and concluding it with an idea that Territorial aggression is often prevented or minimized with early socialization and good control. Young dogs should be taught to take a seat and receive a gift as each new person involves the door. To scale back potential fear and anxiety toward visitors, you ought to make sure that a good sort of visitors come across to go to the puppy while the puppy is young and developing its social skills. In time, most dogs will begin to alert the family by barking when strangers come to the house. However, the well-socialized dog and under good control are often trained to quickly calm down and relax.

CHAPTER SEVEN: "OVERCOMING SEPERATION ANXIETY"

It is unclear why some puppies are more prone to separation anxiety than others. McConnell considers that there may be many reasons, such as those found in some abandoned shelter dogs. Even a traumatic event where there is no owner, like a house burglary. He suggests that personality can play a role, that sticking dogs may be more at risk than independent ones. Other triggers to consider include a sudden change of schedule, a new home, or a sudden absence of a family member, which can include life changes such as divorce, death in the family, or a college-going child. Recent research has pointed to a lack of daily exercise as a potential cause. Because there are many potential triggers for separation anxiety.

Puppy grabbing your car keys and walk towards the front door. You hear all the familiar sounds of dog tags, and then you look down to see sad, shimmering eyes. Your heart lowers. You imagine yourself and tears streaming down your cheeks. You question yourself. Should I take my dog with myself? Puppy parents are as bad as they want to be with their dog sitting and heartbroken, and they need to contact the dog lingo to help with the separation tension. The goal of helping a dog cope with separation anxiety is to make it more comfortable for parents when they leave and learn to enjoy their time alone. Dogs want to protect the people they love, and your dog can enjoy your home by barking at every animal such as rats, cats or any person present around him. It is natural for dogs to warn their parents that barking is not related to separation anxiety if you observe this behavior while you are at it. If your dog is barking or screaming alone when it is alone, it is a sign of separation anxiety. Barking or howling usually comes with at least one sign of separation tension. Dogs scream to get attention or interact with another animal. Screaming is a sound that will stir our hearts. As a dog parent, we all know that after a long day at home, finding kitchen trash can be flipped upside down or a new sofa pillow can be reduced to a pile of white stuffing. Although some destructive behavior is as a dog parent, we all know that after a long day at home, finding kitchen trash can be flipped upside down or a new sofa pillow can be reduced to a pile of white stuffing. Some dogs suffer so much when their parents leave, they can take any step to escape. They can dig in the doors, jump over the fence or escape from the areas where they are alone. If a dog is occupied with fun toys or feels calm and ready for sleep, they will not feel the need to rocket out of your home or yard. On the other hand, a dog may try to back off. They are afraid of the sounds as you leave. They feel lonely or bored. They feel the need to find you and be with you every time. If he escapes to find you, they should not be far from home. This can still be a very critical situation.

Although each species has something unique to cheer about, whether they are excellent hunters, some species are more worrisome than others. On a similar note, external factors can also affect anxiety levels. So, what are some of the causes of dogs with separation anxiety? Although this is a general list, it may help you to understand the possibilities: Smaller dogs seem to have more anxiety than larger breeds. Smaller dogs are found to be less obedient than larger dogs, and owners are generally more enthusiastic and more enthusiastic as they are less consistent when it comes to training smaller dogs. Separation anxiety is more common in dogs who have experienced abandonment, trauma or loss in their lives. Separation anxiety is more common in dogs who are never alone.

Have you ever become nervy about a messy situation, or were you waiting for good or bad news to stop at a fast pace? For the same reason, our puppy speed can help relieve the stress of being separated from parents. However, some dogs may be agitated for other reasons related to separation anxiety. Some dogs may speed up in anticipation of a feast or a fun activity, or because they have to be let out. Older dogs sometimes get upset because of cognitive impairment. If speeding behavior sounds strange to you, it never hurts to evaluate your puppy by a professional. If your dog only speeds when you are not present at home, it may be due to separation anxiety. They either speed back and forth in lines or continue to circle in circles.

Sometimes our they do things we don't understand. One of those things is coprophagy (the word is derived from the Greek which means "feces" and "to eat") is common in many dog homes. Coprophagy may also be the result of an intestinal infection, pancreatitis, or malabsorption of nutrients (in which case the dog may feel chronically hungry and therefore eats the feces to fill up) or when a dog eats their excrement. It's natural phenomena for dogs to want to eat fresh feces because they can find ancestral instincts to protect the pack from intestinal parasites. However, sometimes a dog will get into this stinking habit when worried. Here's how to say if coprophagy is a symptom of separation anxiety rather than instinct. Loneliness or anxiety triggers coprophagy. The dog has accidents when you are far home, but there are no such things happen when you are present at home this is also a very important point that over time they start to love with you and do not do strange things when you are present at home.

You can tell immediately if your puppy is nervous. Their stress is manifested in the physical symptoms you immediately recognize. However, the suffering is usually much worse in the first 15 minutes after you leave. So, you may not be aware of your dog's separation anxiety. Signs of fear such as an increase in heart rate, anxiety, saliva, and anxious behavior. It's hard to imagine your puppy feeling depressed when you leave, but there's no need to worry about it. Our purpose is to help you and your puppy to work through the separation anxiety.

When you reach home, it can be difficult to want to open your arms for your puppy and let him kiss you a lot. As dog parents, we may experience a little separation anxiety from time to time, and it is normal to feel joy in reuniting. However, your pup's extreme enthusiasm can indicate a deeper problem.

Some puppies need a good toy to keep them busy and forget their difficulties. Dog toys can help distract a puppy from your absence and provide mental stimulation and anxiety relief. If your puppy is entertaining and comfortable, they are less likely to focus on the fact that you are not at home.

It can also be helpful to create a room or area where your dog is safe and comfortable. That way, when you are not at home, they can relax and not let fear get out of control.

If he is not playing with toys when you are away maybe, he is worried, or bored. They cannot wait until you come home to remove their worries. He became very excited when you return and follow you everywhere you go when you are at home.

Training a stubborn dog can be difficult at times. Many pet owners feel like they are losing their nerves and almost give up on training the dog. It makes the trainer extremely depressed and stressed when dogs do not leave their bad habits at all. It is difficult for some dogs to understand their trainer because every dog has a different temperament. In this situation, the trainer should not get worried or tensed because to train a dog with such temperament you should not lose your nerves and all you have to do is try a different method of approach to training which also gets interesting for the dog as well and the dog participates in it actively.

When a dog does not listen to their trainer it does not mean that the dog is hardheaded or stubborn and untrainable. This means that normal dog behavior does not always comply with human standards of good manners. Dogs can not adapt like human beings and it will take time for dogs to adapt and they will take time to understand what their trainer wants from them.

In the beginning, the dogs are hesitant and reluctant with their trainers. They do not go out with their trainers for a simple walk and do not obey and follow instructions. To deal with such the nature of dogs you have to take things slow. Start developing a bond by giving small rewarding treats to the dog to appreciate their efforts. If your dog understands that the training part is good than the dog will start complying on trainers' other training and the trainer can train the dog further. Increase the level of difficulty in training by either adding distractions in the training or by changing the types of training. Keep in mind to only change one variable at a time in the training. Otherwise, the training will get too hard for the dog and the dog will start giving up on the training and so will the trainer start give up on the training of the dog.

To train the dog in a good environment is important. You have to choose the location very wisely to train your dog. You have to choose a distraction-free location for your dog. Choose a location that has very fewer distractions, for example, it should not contain food or toys near the training area or it will distract the dog every time you send the dog near it for training. The dog might leave the training to start playing with the toys or start eating the food. You need a completely distraction-free place to train your dog. Even a well train dog can be distracted by other animals such as cats and squirrels or cats or loud sounds.

Keep this thing in mind to reward the dog only for the same set of habits. If you or other members of your family will reward the dog on different occasions on habits that contradict each other then the dog will get stubborn because the dog will get confused in choosing between the right habits to adapt to make the trainer satisfied. Therefore always reward the dog for the same kind of habits.

Avoid punishing the dog. Punishment to a dog at very early stages (even after some time) will induce a feeling of insecurity and fear and anxiety. Punishments usually deteriorate the bond with the dog very negatively and lead the dog into the loophole of insecurity. Trust is not easier to build with dogs if it is broken once. In the long term, this behavior might change to aggression. Avoid such kind of training but try to adopt a reward-based training that will provide the dogs the things they desire in return for completing the training or being a nice dog.

Make sure you reward the dog with the right kind of rewards. If your reward is of very low value to the dog then your dog might not be able to respond to your calls as it used to because it will leave your dog very disinterested in the training. Different diets have different impacts on the dogs' mental and physical health, as explained in the later chapters. To reward your dog you can do other things than just feeding your dog with treats. You can spend some playtime with a dog or play with your favorite toy or play a favorite game with the dog.

If he cannot live without you, they may experience great anxiety during your absence. It's hard to know your dog is suffering from anxiety and, naturally, you want to do anything to help them. You may also consider anti-anxiety medications for your dog. Every day is different. Some people may not take the medication properly, but others may benefit greatly. Some medications should only be used for a long time, others only as needed. It is always best to consult a veterinarian before giving any medication to your dog. Also, consult a veterinarian to rule out other causes of anxious behavior. Just as there are many remedies for tension in people, dogs also have different types of tension solutions. Some medicines are prescribed or available over the counter, while others are considered natural remedies. For something less serious, it might be good enough to relax and relax your puppy when you leave home alone. Check out various anti-anxiety options that can help you find the best medicine for your dog.

If separation anxiety has a grip on your furlough, it may be time to consult a doctor and find out if a prescription medication is the best option. Combining the right medication with coping skills can help you live your puppy without worry. Also, when you step outside the door, you will be less concerned about knowing that your dog is content, safe and okay if you are not.

It is important to practice gradual separation and slowly develop the stamina to own your dog. Choose a time to practice while you and your dog are calm and relaxed. Baby gates can be used at doorsteps to teach your dog that you can stay away from him without worrying. He can see you, hear you, marry you, but not physically connect with you. Before you go through the Baby Cat dispersal, find some treats on the ground to search for your dog, or play with him as a toy, chew or food release toy. He'll learn that it's not okay to be alone because he'll have a good time! If you don't have a baby gate, don't worry, just close the door slowly, but be aware that you are completely out of sight, so this is a big step. Get out only for a very short time to start. Start with very short periods and then gradually build up the time you are away from your dog until he is relaxed. Gradually increase the time before you return to the room. If your dog is worried or shows signs of anxiety, try to stay near the gate if you are using one, or leave him alone for a short time. If he is unable to cope with this level of separation, contact a qualified behavioral specialist for guidance.

It's best to keep your puppy comfortable when he is alone at home. Make a table for your puppy and make sure your family sticks to it. Always give your puppy a chance to go back to normal before raising him. Train your pup to crate. When done properly, using a crate is a great way to keep your puppy calm and out of trouble! See our guide to training your puppy for more information. Crate him for a short while you are at it. For example, when you watch TV, put your puppy in his cage and put the cage next to the sofa. Graded time will gradually increase. The reward for peaceful behavior with quiet praise. Start leaving your puppy alone in his cage. Start with a few minutes at a time. Gradually increase the time spent alone. Limit the attention he receives shortly before departure, so it is not such a shock when your family leaves. When your puppy is out of his nest, stay calm and keep the greetings to a minimum. You don't want to encourage him. Most puppies do not need to be fostered for the rest of their lives, but do not rush to freedom. Generally, puppies are not ready to provide unsupervised independence in your home until approximately one and a half years of age. Try to make sure that someone in your family is at home as much as possible. Consider hiring a puppy-walker or neighbor to give your puppy a lunch break when everyone is at work or school. Keeping your schedule consistent over the weekend can help make things easier for your puppy.

CHAPTER EIGHT: "DIET & NUTRITION"

Dogs are one of the most common pets around the world independent of their breed and size. Just like every other mammal, dogs need proper diet and nutrition for a healthy life. And for a pet dog, the nutrition and diet are controlled by its master. Dogs need several kinds of nutrients to survive including amino acids, minerals, proteins, carbohydrates, fatty acids, vitamins, and water most essentially. Dogs cannot survive without proteins in their daily diet, as proteins are the building blocks of fibers and muscles in the living body. Dietary proteins contain 10 specific amino acids that dogs cannot build inside their bodies. Similarly, Dietary fats are of great significance in their diet. Fats are mostly extracted from seed oils and animal fats mostly. Fats including fatty acid play a vital role in cell structure formation and function. Food fats tend to develop the taste and texture of the dog's food. EFA (Essential Fatty Acids) are required to keep the dog's skin and coat healthy.

Dogs require a certain amount of energy in their body to get involved in normal daily life activities. Growth, exercise, pregnancy, and lactation generally increase energy requirements. And this energy comes from carbohydrates, proteins, and fats which are only derived from food and supplements. A growing puppy needs about twice as many calories per pound of body weight as an adult dog of the same breed. In the first four weeks of birth, the puppy only needs breastfeeding. But after 4 weeks it starts needing food because the mother's milk is no longer providing sufficient energy. Puppy dogs were grown and develop soft teeth by the age of 5 weeks. These teeth help them chew soft food in the beginning. A growing puppy needs a lot of energy which is only harvested from food. Three times a day is preferred as the metabolism is fast. Giant breeds (like Danes) require to start needing food at a very early age because of the smaller digestive tracts. The energy harvested from milk to completely fulfill the growth requirements is not enough, so these dogs are fed 2 times a day to entertain their body requirement. Puppies 6 months and younger should eat three to four times a day. At 6 months, they can eat twice daily. Once pups become adults, they can get one or two meals a day, depending on how much exercise they get daily. Smaller breeds have a faster metabolism which means that they consume more energy than others depending upon their body conditions and activity level. While larger breeds have slower metabolism but of course they possess larger appetites. For larger breeds, heavy kibbles are prepared that encourage the dogs to chew for a long time and these kibbles provide protein-rich nutrients. Lazy dogs burn less amount of energy so it is alright to feed them with a light diet to avoid weight gain.

Dogs are choosy over their food and they might avoid certain food that lacks the nutrients a dog needs. The attitude of the dog depends on the food given by the master. Dogs mostly like to eat protein and fat-rich meals which include meat. Many health issues can arise from an unbalanced diet and this can also lead to the behavioral issues of dogs. For example, a dog suffering from a disorder in the urinary tract because of its diet may get stressed out or annoyed due to pain and discomfort. Millions of biochemical reactions take place simultaneously inside a living body so it is very essential for a dog to have a balanced diet and maintain good health. In case of an inadequate amount of diet, a dog stays hungry all the time and may get itself involved in disruptive behavior commonly scavenging and eating feces. We can see stray dogs near dustbin and trash yards where they can find foods. Similarly, a pet can also engage itself in these activities if it is not fed adequately and get itself infected from polluted things. Canines who are dissatisfied with their diet because it lacks certain nutrients can also lead to a condition known as pica. This thing can lead the dog's strong desire to eat non-food items such as soil and plants.

Free feeding means feeding a dog once a day or leaving food out all day long so the dog can eat whenever it wants to, is not recommended at all. Feeding the dog 2 or 3 times a day with a well spacing is preferred. It helps the dog to digest the previous meal before taking the next one. And it prevents the dog to get any digestive disorder, hence the behavior of the dog does not go in bad terms. According to researches and studies, there are antioxidants in dog foods that are good for the brain. Older dogs getting antioxidants in their diet are most likely to learn and perform a task given by their master in a shorter period as compared to dogs who do not get these nutrients. Studies show that older dogs with healthy diets are less likely to undergo age-related attitude changes associated with cognitive decline and egoistic nature. Besides triggering a good mood and positive attitude, good nutrition also keeps the dog's metabolism good and immune system working properly.

Dogs, unlike cats, are not strict carnivores. While meat makes up most of its diet as it contains fats and proteins, domestic dogs can also get carbohydrates, fruits, and vegetables. This non-meat diet is not only contaminated but can be an important source of vitamins, minerals, and fiber. Good dog food will contain meat, vegetables, grains, and fruits. The best dog food contains the highest types of ingredients that are ideal for your dog's digestive system. Dogs can be trained anyway, they can eat vegetables and some dry fruits as well. Dogs eat sweet edibles with great desire including cookies, biscuit, and chews but it should not exceed 10% of the daily food plan. Cocking chocolate is fatal to the dog, it not a good decision to give a chocolate bar to a dog. Dog's digestive system is different from the human digestive system because human food is often too salty or protein-rich which may prove to be bad for a dog's health in long term eating. Human food does not satisfy the mineral and essential nutrients requirement of dogs commonly. Raw meat seems like a natural food for a dog but it can contain bacteria that can be very harmful to the dog. Dogs love to eat soft bones but small pieces of bone and fish bones should not be fed, because they can damage the teeth and cause blockage in the throat or intestines. Chicken bones should always be avoided because they can be swallowed by chewing and can cause real damage when swallowed, although they are traditionally fed to dogs. If the dog is getting a nutritious and fully balanced diet then there is no necessity to give the dog extra supplements.

During pregnancy, dogs must be taking everything it needs to stay healthy and keep the puppies alive inside its body. Eating right makes sure that the mother's dog and its offspring are healthy and happy, otherwise, it can prove to be very wrong for both the mother and its children. The mother dog needs extra supplements to provide energy to its offspring. High-quality puppy food is preferred as it contains larger amounts of every nutrient required. When feeding pregnant dogs it must be kept in mind they do not overeat in the first few weeks of pregnancy. During the early stages, the female dog may go off its food or may experience nausea or vomiting. But this is very normal and dogs are not to be forced to eat. Around the 5th week, the diet has to be increased gradually as there are one or more puppies inside the mother who are alive as well and need a certain amount of nutrients. Overeating may cause the dog to become lazy and obese which can lead to a problem during pregnancy and labor. It is better to feed the mother dog little and often so it gets time to digest and does not become obese.

In a lifetime a dog can get some of the common diseases for short periods. Many dogs get kennel cough which is the common name for *canine infection tracheobronchitis.* It is a respiratory disorder/infection in dogs caused by bacteria and viruses. Harsh coughing is a common symptom of kennel cough. The illness can be caused by several different bacteria and viruses, and sometimes a combination of both. Dogs become infected when they inhale these bacteria or virus particles into their respiratory tract. The most common cause is a bacteria strain called Bordetella Bronchiseptica, which is why some people call kennel cough Bordetella. But dogs are more likely to be infected by Bordetella when their immune system is weakened, usually by an infection from a virus. Some viruses known to make dogs more susceptible to kennel cough include canine adenovirus, canine distemper virus, canine herpes, parainfluenza virus, and canine reovirus. Kennel cough usually goes away by itself - in most cases, it clears within three weeks and requires no treatment. If your dog feels dangerous and eats well, you should be able to use home remedies to make your dog more comfortable. This includes keeping them in a humid area and avoid using collars.

Dog's training is the most important factor that decides the behavior of the dog towards its master. Dogs are greedy and always want to have something between their jaws, this can help us train them. Dogs can perform a task to get food from their master, a master can develop a sense of understanding with his dog by awarding him with something the dog can eat. Gradually the dog learns to co-operate with its master and be able to listen and act upon the objective provided by its master. Training depends upon the breed of dog, some breeds are stubborn and do not perform a task easily but it is not impossible to train them. Awarding a dog when it performs a task will help him understand his master. Meatballs are common for this purpose as they are small and tasty. Setting rules and regulations will help the dog to understand the master. For example, if the dog is not allowed to sit over the tables, he should be called over and over again to leave that place and when he leaves that place he will get a piece of cookie or a kibble. This will help the dog to understand the master's language.

Rewarding the dog's good behavior is one the best thing to make a dog learn ethics and morals. But it should be kept in mind that training should not let the dog overeat or free eat. Ending the training session with a dog in good terms also helps the dog to get along with his master. At the end of the training, the dog should be given something as a reward either it's a large bone or a cookie or two.

Just like every other living being dogs also require proper meals to stay healthy but as pet dogs are also representative of their home, so they should be kept healthy and trained.

CONCLUSION

In light of the above evidence and facts, it can be stated that puppy training may seem hard, but instead, it is easy. It is a bit technical and due to which, many people tend to fail in it. The significant point in this book is the psychology of the dog. Of course, you need to learn the actions, thought, and desires of dogs to get going with them. In other words, you can't communicate with a person that speaks in a different language; you need a translator. Similarly, to communicate with your dog, you need to learn the dog's psychology. This will boost up the training procedure.

Apart from this, the book holds different tips and tricks that can help your dog in different ways, such as potty training, learning tricks, behavior, and much more. We all know the love of dogs and their cuteness. But, can we pet one? or train one dog? Therefore, to fulfill your dream of having a dog and petting it, it is necessary to give a read to this comprehensive guide.

Very soon you will be walking with your best friend alongside the road!

"Dog lovers know something that no one else does: there's no purer form of love than the kind you get from your four-legged family."

www.ingramcontent.com/pod-product-compliance
Lightning Source LLC
Chambersburg PA
CBHW062140100526
44589CB00014B/1634